The VENISON COOK

106 Imaginative Recipes

Diane and Nicholas Dalton

The Crowood Press

First published in 1991 by
The Crowood Press
Gipsy Lane, Swindon
Wiltshire, SN2 6DQ

British Library Cataloguing in Publication Data

Dalton, Diane
   The venison cook.
   1. Food : Venison dishes. Recipes
   I. Title   II. Dalton, Nicholas

   ISBN 1 85223 470 9

Acknowledgements

Line illustrations and jacket by Matthew Lawrence

Typeset by Keyboard Services, Luton, Beds
Printed in Great Britain at The Bath Press

CONTENTS

INTRODUCTION

In this book, we have tried to dispel the many myths surrounding the cooking of venison. Most traditional recipes stem from Victorian and Edwardian times and advocated heavy, lengthy marinading to render the meat actually edible. If a tough old buck is dragged down from the hill, you can marinade it for weeks and it will still remain the same – a tough old buck. So – forget Mrs Beeton – buy your venison from a reputable game dealer or butcher where you will get a joint of meat correctly hung, which basically needs no marinading to be tender.

Venison is gaining popularity by leaps and bounds in this health-conscious age. It is one of the original free-range, additive-free meats, low in fat and cholesterol but best of all, it is quite delicious to eat.

You will also find it increasingly available in supermarkets, giving a variety of cuts at competitive prices. The recipes in this book will show you how easy and versatile venison is to cook; from family meals and barbecues to more formal entertaining. So, sit down, pour yourself a drink, read the recipes and enjoy a new experience in gastronomy.

CHAPTER 1

SPECIES AND PREPARATION

SPECIES

There are six species of wild deer in the British Isles: red, roe, fallow, sika, muntjac and Chinese water deer.

Red deer are found predominantly in Scotland, in woodland and mountain areas. These are the classic 'monarch of the glen', much photographed in Victorian times and the largest species. A mature stag can weigh between 90–190kg (200–400lb). The meat is dark and very lean and the majority of venison joints in supermarkets are from red deer. It is also very popular on the continent. Due to the recent upsurge of interest in low fat, low cholesterol meat, many deer farms have sprung up over the country. Red deer form the majority species on these farms.

Roe deer weigh about 20–30kg (50–60lb) on the hoof and are found in large quantities in the south of England. They are pushing their way up towards the Midlands and are common in East Anglia, northern England and most of Scotland. Wales has none. Much prized on the continent, roe venison is a fine-grained meat and, with its delicate flavour is perhaps the most popular of all in the United Kingdom.

Fallow deer can weigh up to 80kg (150lb) but a beast of this weight has seen the sun set too many times to be worth anything apart from being the principle ingredient of game pie. In good supply at your local game dealer, fallow venison will generally be cut from does and prickets (young bucks), will taste faintly like beef and be very tender. Generally, wild deer do not have a high fat content, but fallow are an exception. They have a knack of living off the fat of the land and especially in late summer and autumn are well larded to give extra-succulent joints.

Sika deer are quite scarce in England, and are found only around the New Forest, Dorset and northern England. In Scotland they are quite numerous, most being shot in Forestry Commission woods and exported. They are about the size of fallow deer and the flavour is quite delicious, so if you are ever offered some, grab the opportunity to sample it.

Chinese water deer are confined only to a small part of England between Bedford and Norfolk. This species, together with the muntjac, was introduced to Woburn Abbey in recent years, and many have escaped into the surrounding area. They are unlikely to be found for sale in any quantity, so we must look to other species to provide us with readily available venison for the table.

CULLING AND SEASONS

There is a strict procedure adhered to in Scotland and England for culling the various species at appropriate seasons. This is worked out to avoid the time when the does are with young, and also to maintain the balance of population number in any particular herd or community.

Seasons in England and Wales

Red Deer:	Stags, 1 August–30 April.
	Hinds, 1 November–28 February.
Fallow deer:	Bucks, 1 August–30 April.
	Does, 1 November–28 February.
Roe deer:	Bucks, 1 April–31 October.
	Does, 1 November–28 February.

Seasons in Scotland

Red deer:	Stags, 1 July–20 October.
	Hinds, 21 October–15 February.
Fallow deer:	Bucks, 1 August–30 April.
	Does, 21 October–15 February.
Roe deer:	Bucks, 1 April–20 October.
	Does, 21 October–31 March.

PREPARATION OF MEAT

It is essential that all venison culled is gralloched as soon as possible. The carcass is then hung for a period of 5–14 days to bring out the natural flavour of the meat. It is then skinned and jointed for the table.
Suitable for roasting: joints from the saddle, haunch or shoulder.
Suitable for pot roasting: joints from haunch or shoulder.
Suitable for casseroles: cuts from shoulder, flank or haunch.
Suitable for grilling and frying: loin chops, fillet or haunch steaks.

CHAPTER 2

MARINADING

Forget any older recipes for heavy, lengthy marinades as these will drown the flavour of the venison – you might just as well marinade your shoes. The secret of a good marinade is always to let the taste of the meat come through. The basic marinade below is a marinade we recommend for all cuts and methods of cooking. The juniper berries give a splendid, aromatic flavour, so try to buy them if possible.

Basic Marinade

4 tablespoons of as good a quality of
  oil as possible
2 tablespoons red wine – if no excuse
  to open a bottle, then the
  equivalent of dry sherry or even red
  wine vinegar will do
1 teaspoon grated lemon rind
¼ teaspoon freshly grated nutmeg
1 tablespoon juniper berries, crushed
½ clove of garlic, crushed
salt and pepper

Combine all the ingredients and beat well or shake in a screw-top jar. The marinade will keep in the refrigerator for weeks and can be increased or decreased in proportional quantities.

Spicy Marinade

This is excellent for chops, liver or rump steaks – especially for barbecues as it has a more robust, 'peasanty' feel for al-fresco meals. To the basic marinade add:

1 dessert spoon tomato purée
1 dessert spoon soy sauce
1 level teaspoon dry mustard powder
1 teaspoon brown sugar

SOUPS

The secret of all successful soups is of course, a rich stock. For a good venison stock you need to bribe or cajole your local gamekeeper into saving some venison bones for you.

Venison Stock

venison bones
1 clove garlic, crushed
dash of oil
1.1l/2 pints water

1. Put all the venison bones in a roasting tin and add the garlic and oil.

2 Roast in a medium oven for about 30 minutes or until you can smell the aroma. At this point, pour the water over the stock bones and return to the oven for 10 minutes.

3 Strain off the liquid into a saucepan and simmer for 1 hour.

4 Refrigerate until required.

Rich Game Soup

Serves 6

550ml/1 pint venison stock
225g/½lb minced casserole venison
100g/¼lb minced pheasant or pigeon
*   meat*
1 small chopped onion, carrot and
*   stick of celery*
1 tablespoon tomato purée
dash of oil
chopped parsley to garnish

---

1 Fry the meats in the oil, stirring carefully for about 5 minutes.

---

2 Add the chopped vegetables, tomato purée and stock. Bring slowly to the boil
and then simmer gently for about 1 hour.

---

3 Garnish with chopped parsley and season well.

Cream of Venison Soup with Watercress and Courgette

Serves 4

This is an unusual soup which can be served hot or cold.

550ml/1 pint venison stock
100g/¼lb cooked venison, minced
2 courgettes, roughly chopped
1 bunch watercress, washed
    thoroughly
½ chopped onion
150ml/¼ pint single cream
dash of oil
croutons or watercress to garnish

---

1 Fry the chopped vegetables in a little oil until tender. Add the venison and stir well, then add the watercress and turn quickly in the resultant juices.

---

2 Add the stock and then liquidise the whole lot until smooth – the venison will give it 'texture'.

---

3 To serve hot, stir in the cream at the last moment and add wholemeal croutons. To serve cold, swirl the cream into individual bowls and garnish with watercress.

Curried Venison and Parsnip Soup

Serves 4

This is definitely a winter soup. It improves with keeping, so prepare it the day before the first frosts are forecast.

550ml/1 pint venison stock
100g/4oz cooked venison, minced
½ chopped onion
1 large parsnip, peeled and chopped
1 tablespoon curry powder
dash of oil

1 Gently fry all the solid ingredients in a little oil. Add the curry powder and stock, and stir well.

2 Put it all into the liquidiser until smooth and creamy. If the soup seems too thick, then thin down with a little milk.

3 Serve really hot with French bread or big, chunky doorsteps of granary bread.

Winter Soup with Lentils and Tomato

Serves 4

This is a real rib-sticking soup – a meal in itself.

550ml/1 pint venison stock
100g/¼lb minced, cooked venison
  meat
100g/¼lb minced cooked venison
  liver or kidney
1 tin of tomatoes (large)
225g/½lb red or green lentils
pinch dried thyme

1 Cook lentils in a little water for about 10 minutes until tender. Drain and set aside.

2 Pour stock into a saucepan, add the venison meat and liver or kidney, the tin of tomatoes and the cooked lentils. Season well, add the thyme and simmer gently for about 30 minutes.

3 Serve straight from the pot with slices of French bread covered in French mustard and quickly grilled.

CHAPTER 4

ROASTING

Great care must be taken when roasting venison so that it does not become too dry during the cooking time. Venison has very little fat and therefore must be kept lubricated whilst cooking. The best way to do this is to wrap the joint in a loose parcel of oiled or buttered foil. This retains all the succulent juices and acts as a self-baster, so you can forget about the meat once it is in the oven.

Basic Roast Haunch

Serves 6–8

*1 haunch (2–3kg/4–6lb), or
1 boneless haunch joint (about
    1½–2kg/3–4lb)
sheet of oiled foil to wrap joint in
basic marinade*

Pre-heat the oven to 180°C/325°F/Gas Mark 4.

---

1 Pour marinade over meat and baste at intervals. Leave it overnight or from 3–12 hours, depending on how well organised you are.

---

2 When ready for cooking, lift from the marinade and place onto oiled foil, keeping the juniper berries on the meat. Wrap it in a loose parcel and roast it in a slow to medium oven allowing 20 minutes for every ½kg or 1lb.

---

3 When serving, use all the meat juices together with the marinade for the gravy. Serve with rowanberry jelly or redcurrant jelly. Make sure the plates are really hot – venison has almost no fat and cools very quickly.

Saddle with Plums and Almonds

Serves 4–6

This sounds the most unlikely combination of ingredients, but it is well worth the effort and produces a thick, rich sauce with a 'what on earth is in it' flavour.

1 saddle (1½–2kg/3–4lb)
2 bay leaves
sprig fresh thyme
25g/1oz chopped, blanched almonds
225g/8oz ripe black plums
25g/1oz large raisins, soaked for
*   1 hour in water*
½ cup red wine
4 grated ginger nut biscuits
25g/1oz arrowroot or cornflour
oiled foil
basic marinade

Pre-heat oven to 190°C/375°F/Gas Mark 5

---

1 Marinade saddle for 3–12 hours. Cook plums until tender, remove stones and purée flesh in blender.

---

2 Place venison in centre of oiled foil with bay leaves and fresh thyme. Cook in medium oven for 1 hour.

---

3 Remove meat and keep in warm place. Reduce the marinade over a high flame. Add plum purée, drained raisins and red wine and stir well. Sprinkle on arrowroot or cornflour and stir again. Now add the grated ginger biscuits and cook slowly for 10 minutes.

---

4 Dish the joint for carving on a very hot plate, serve the sauce separately and wait for the compliments.

Saddle with Cream and Port

Serves 4–6

A Czech recipe from Maryna Klimentova.

1 saddle
1 of each chopped – onion, celery,
*   carrot, green pepper*
150ml/5fl oz double cream
small wine glass of port
1 tablespoon of oil

Pre-heat oven to 190°C/375°F/Gas Mark 5.

1 Season the saddle with salt and pepper and place in a roasting tin. Cover with the chopped vegetables and drizzle over the oil. Cover all of this with a sheet of foil and roast for about 1½ hours.

2 When cooked (it should be pinkish, but if you do not care for this then cook all the way through) remove the saddle from the oven and keep hot. Put the roasting tin on top of the stove over a high heat, add the port and stir round to incorporate all the meat juices and vegetables. Keep this warm while you carve the meat.

3 At the last minute, add all the cream to the sauce mixture and serve a spoonful over each portion. The double cream makes this recipe extra special, so forget the calories for once and indulge yourself.

Saddle with Tansy and Rosemary

Serves 4–6

A recipe for the early summer – try hard to find fresh herbs for an exquisite flavour.

1 saddle
handful of fresh tansy leaves
6 sprigs fresh rosemary
25g/1oz unsalted butter
1 tablespoon olive oil

Pre-heat oven to 190°C/375°F/Gas Mark 5.

1 Season the saddle, dot with butter and pour over the oil. Scatter the herbs over the joint, wrap it all in a loose foil parcel and bake in a medium oven for 1–1½ hours.

2 Serve with new potatoes and a fresh green salad.

Saddle with Piquant Sauce

Serves 4–6

1 saddle
1 chopped onion
1 chopped carrot
50g/2oz chopped ham
1 tablespoon oil
1 bay leaf
pinch fresh chopped thyme
pinch fresh chopped parsley
1 tablespoon wine vinegar
1 tablespoon wholegrain mustard
275ml/½ pint venison or other meat
    stock

Pre-heat oven to 190°C/375°F/Gas Mark 5.

---

1   Roast the saddle in a loose oiled foil parcel for about 1–1½ hours. Meanwhile make the stunning sauce.

---

2   Fry the vegetables and ham in the oil until tender. Add the mustard and wine vinegar, stir in the stock and the herbs and simmer the whole mixture for about 30 minutes.

---

3   When ready, carve the meat and serve the sauce separately. This is good with a purée of potatoes and with broccoli.

Fillet en Crôute with Chestnut Purée

Serves 4

The beauty of this rather impresive recipe is that you can prepare it the night before.

1 fillet
225g/½lb puff pastry
1 tin chestnut purée
100g/¼lb sliced mushrooms
milk to glaze

Pre-heat oven to 200°C/400°F/Gas Mark 6.

---

1 Roll out the pastry into a rectangle about 2in/5cm larger all round than the fillet. Place the fillet on the pastry, cover with the chestnut purée and top with sliced mushrooms.

---

2 Season well, fold the pastry up to cover the fillet, using a little milk to seal the pastry casing. If possible, refrigerate overnight.

---

3 When ready, brush pastry with a little milk, place in hot oven and cook for 40 minutes.

---

4 Serve in thick slices with glazed carrots and a green vegetable.

Haunch with Rich Orange Sauce

Serves 6–8

1 haunch (1½–2kg/3–4lb)
basic marinade
4 oranges – Seville if possible
1 tablespoon clear honey
1 tablespoon red wine
1 tablespoon crushed juniper berries
dash of cooking oil
150ml/¼ pint water or game stock

Pre-heat oven to 190°C/375°F/Gas Mark 5.

1 Marinade the venison haunch overnight in a basic marinade.

2 Lift from the marinade and roast in a loose parcel of oiled foil for about 1½ hours. When cooked, squeeze the juice from 1 orange over the joint and keep warm.

3 While the meat is roasting, prepare the sauce. Coarsely chop 2 oranges and add to the stock and wine in a small saucepan. Add the crushed juniper berries and simmer gently for about 20 minutes. Pour in the honey and boil fiercely for ½ a minute to reduce the sauce slightly. Strain through a sieve and keep hot in a sauce boat.

4 Serve the joint on a large hot dish garnished with orange slices from the last orange and with the orange sauce passed around separately.

Note: If you are in a hurry or running very late, you can make a simpler sauce using bitter orange marmalade diluted in a little red wine and stock. Bring it to the boil as described earlier and reduce for a few seconds, while you sip the rest of the wine to calm you down.

Roast Haunch with Onion and Mushroom Sauce

Serves 6–8

1 haunch (1½–2kg/3–4lb)
basic marinade
2 onions, finely chopped
100g/¼lb mushrooms, finely
*   chopped*
1 teaspoon grated nutmeg
1 dessert spoon flour
275ml/½ pint rich game stock or
*   consommé*
1 clove garlic, crushed
dash of oil

Pre-heat oven to 190°C/375°F/Gas Mark 5.

1 Marinade the venison and roast in oiled foil for about 1½ hours. Meanwhile make this unusual sauce.

2 Fry the chopped onion in the oil until golden brown, add the mushrooms and fry for a further 2 or 3 minutes. Stir in the flour, stock or consommé, garlic and nutmeg and season well. Bring gently to the boil as it thickens and simmer gently to infuse the flavours.

3 Carve the venison haunch in fairly thin slices on a very hot plate and pour over the sauce before serving.

4 This recipe goes well with cooked pasta as an accompaniment instead of the usual potatoes.

Stuffed, Boned Haunch with Chestnuts

Serves 6–8

This recipe has such an unusual and subtle blend of flavours, that we recommend not to marinade the meat first.

1 boned haunch
275g/¾lb chestnuts, peeled and left
    whole
1 sliced onion
2 carrots, sliced lengthwise
pinch of dried thyme
1 clove garlic, crushed
50g/2oz unsalted butter
salt and pepper

Pre-heat oven to 180°C/350°F/Gas Mark 4.

1 Fresh chestnuts are imperative – they are fiddly to do, but you can prepare them beforehand when there is something good to listen to on the radio. Give them a 20-minute simmer in boiling water before peeling and they should not cause too much stress.

2 Lay out the boned haunch on a sheet of oiled foil and season well. Put the chestnuts, onion and carrots in layers along the length of the meat. Sprinkle on the herbs and garlic and dot with 25g/1oz of the butter.

3 Using string, tie the joint into a manageable roll, dot with the remaining butter and season again with salt and lots of ground black pepper. Wrap the whole parcel in oiled foil and roast for about 2 hours.

4 Unwrap and pour off the juices into a warmed saucepan. When ready to serve, slice the joint straight across in fairly thick slices and pour over the buttery, herby juices.

5 Best served with a simple green salad and baked potatoes.

Boned Haunch with Dijon Mustard

Serves 6–8

A good winter roast.

1 boned haunch
2 tablespoons wholegrain mustard
1 clove crushed garlic
2 tablespoons redcurrant jelly
salt and pepper

Pre-heat oven to 190°C/375°F/Gas Mark 5.

1 Season the boned meat. Spread with 1 tablespoon of wholegrain mustard, 1 tablespoon of the redcurrant jelly, garlic and salt and pepper.

2 Tie loosely with string and place on oiled foil. Cover the outside of the joint with the rest of the mustard and redcurrant jelly. Wrap the whole lot in the oiled foil and roast for about 2 hours.

3 This is good served with roast potatoes and red cabbage.

Roast Shoulder of Venison

Serves 4

A roast shoulder is one of the sweetest of the roasting cuts and also the cheapest. The roe shoulder is small and will feed only 2–3 people, but the fallow will feed 4 people easily.

1 fallow shoulder
basic marinade
1 clove garlic
1 dessert spoon fresh chopped thyme
1 dessert spoon fresh chopped lemon
  balm
50g/2oz unsalted butter
grated rind from 1 lemon

Pre-heat oven to 180°C/350°F/Gas Mark 4.

1 Marinade the shoulder overnight.

2 Place onto a square of oiled foil, sprinkle over the herbs, garlic and lemon rind and dot with butter. Season well and wrap in a loose parcel. Roast for about 1 hour.

3 Serve with new potatoes and a selection of summer vegetables.

Shoulder with Rowanberry Glaze

Serves 2

A very simple roast – again delicious summer eating when the roe bucks are in season during July. Substitute with redcurrant jelly if you cannot get rowanberry jelly.

1 good sized roe shoulder
1 tablespoon rowanberry jelly
1 teaspoon grated nutmeg

Pre-heat oven to 180°C/350°F/Gas Mark 4.

1 Spread the joint with the rowanberry jelly and sprinkle over the nutmeg. Season well.

2 Roast for about 1 hour and serve with new potatoes and a green salad with fresh orange segments.

Boned Shoulder with Prunes and Rice

Serves 4–6

1 fallow shoulder, boned
8 large, pitted prunes soaked
overnight
100g/¼lb cooked long grain rice
1 teaspoon chopped parsley
150ml/¼ pint game stock
50g/2oz flour or arrowroot
25g/1oz butter

Pre-heat oven to 180°C/350°F/Gas Mark 4.

1 Flatten out the boned joint. Place the prunes, rice and parsley in the middle and tie the whole joint with string. Wrap in oiled foil and roast for 1½ hours.

2 Melt the butter in a small saucepan, add the flour, stir well and pour on the stock. Bring to the boil and stir well as it thickens.

3 When the joint is cooked, add the meat juices to this sauce and serve separately as you slice the meat.

Shoulder with Potato, Swede and Celeriac

Serves 4

1 fallow shoulder
basic marinade
1kg/2lb potatoes, thinly sliced
1 large root celeriac, thinly sliced
1 small swede, coarsely grated
100g/4oz butter
grated nutmeg

Pre-heat oven to 180°C/350°F/Gas Mark 4.

---

1 Marinade the shoulder overnight.

---

2 Roast on oiled foil for about 1½ hours. Meanwhile make this delicious vegetable accompaniment.

---

3 Butter a casserole dish. Arrange alternate layers of potato, celeriac and swede, season each layer well and dot with the remaining butter. Forget the diet tonight and do not stint on the quantity of butter.

---

4 When all the vegetables are used up, grate a little nutmeg over the top and put it in the oven for about 1 hour.

---

5 When the meat is done, pour a little of the meat juices over the vegetable mixture. Serve a generous helping of vegetable accompaniment with each serving of the sliced meat.

CHAPTER 5
FOIL COOKERY

Because venison is an exceptionally lean meat, it is important to keep it moist when cooking. This is where foil cookery really scores – we recommend it with enthusiasm, 'when in doubt, foil it' being a favourite motto.

Foil-baked Fillet with Mushrooms and Rowanberry Jelly

Serves 4

Pure, gastronomic perfection – try very hard to acquire rowanberry jelly. It has a perfumed bitter-sweet flavour which marries so well with venison – redcurrant jelly may be substituted, but it is a very poor relation.

1 fillet (450–600g/1–1½lb)
1 heaped tablespoon rowanberry jelly
100g/4oz sliced mushrooms
1 dessert spoon crushed juniper
  berries
salt and pepper

Pre-heat oven to 200°C/400°F/Gas Mark 6.

---

1 Season the fillet with salt and pepper and the crushed juniper berries. Spread rowanberry jelly over the top side and place on oiled foil.

---

2 Add the sliced mushrooms and wrap in loose parcel.

---

3 Cook for 30 minutes if you care for pink meat, 45 minutes for beige.

---

4 Slice at the table in thickish slices and serve with a potato purée and one green vegetable.

Fillet with Mixed Peppers

Serves 4

*1 whole fillet or 4 small cut fillet
    steaks*
1 dessert spoon olive oil
*1 of each – red, green and yellow
    peppers, thinly sliced*
*2 shallots or 1 small onion, finely
    chopped*

Pre-heat oven to 200°C/400°F/Gas Mark 6.

---

1 Season the fillets well and lay on top of foil squares.

---

2 Drizzle the olive oil over and scatter a mixture of the green, yellow and red peppers and shallots over each fillet. Wrap loosely in parcels.

---

3 Cook for 20 minutes if individual fillets or 30–40 minutes for a whole fillet.

Fillet Provençale

Serves 4

This is a lovely aromatic recipe with a rich tomato and herb sauce that will remind you of holidays in France. If it does not, then take the holiday in France before you try the recipe or the enjoyment of cooking will not be so evocative.

4 150g/6oz fillet steaks
2 large sliced tomatoes
1 large sliced green pepper
20–24 black, pitted olives
2 cloves crushed garlic
1 tablespoon tomato purée
1 teaspoon dried oregano or basil

Pre-heat oven to 200°C/400°F/Gas Mark 6.

1 Lay each fillet in a square of oiled foil and season well. Spread each fillet with equal portions of tomato purée and garlic, tomatoes, peppers and olives. Add the herbs and wrap in loose parcels.

2 Cook for 20 minutes.

3 Serve each parcel as a portion and let your guests unwrap the meal and all its fragrances as added enjoyment.

Rump Steaks with Courgettes and Mushrooms

Serves 4

4 100–150g/4–6oz rump steaks
4 small courgettes, sliced
225g/½lb thinly sliced mushrooms
50g/2oz unsalted butter
1 teaspoon dried thyme

Pre-heat oven to 190°C/375°F/Gas Mark 5.

1 Lay each fillet on a square of buttered foil – use all the butter and forget the calories. This recipe cannot tolerate a substitute, so do not insult it by using polyunsaturated chemicals.

2 Season well and scatter on each fillet an equal portion of courgettes, mushroom and thyme. Cook for 20 minutes

3 Serve as individual parcels with baked potatoes and salad.

Rump Steaks with Curd Cheese and Chives

Serves 4

Try this recipe in summer when you can actually get fresh chives – dried chives are not a good substitute.

4 rump steaks
225g/½lb curd cheese
2 dessert spoons fresh chopped chives
2 cloves garlic, crushed

Pre-heat oven to 190°C/375°F/Gas Mark 5.

1 Lay each fillet on a square of oiled foil, spread with the curd cheese, chives and garlic. Bake for 20 minutes.

2 This is especially good served hot with risotto or cold with a rice salad.

Rump Steaks with Apple and Prunes

Serves 4

For lovers of 'sweet and sour' flavours, this is an unusual recipe which is also very successful on the barbecue.

4 rump steaks
12 large pitted prunes
150ml/¼ pint thick apple purée
1 tablespoon wine vinegar
pinch of grated nutmeg

Pre-heat oven to 190°C/375°F/Gas Mark 5.

---

1 Lay each steak on a square of oiled foil. Spread with apple purée, top each steak with four prunes and season with a little grated nutmeg and the wine vinegar.

---

2 Cook for 20 minutes.

Steak and Ham 'Sandwiches'

Serves 4

This is an unusual combination of textures and flavours without the hassle of long-term preparation. It can be prepared the night before and refrigerated until needed.

1lb rump steak
8 slices thinly cut ham
¼lb cream of curd cheese
¼lb thinly sliced mushrooms

Pre-heat oven to 190°C/375°F/Gas Mark 5.

---

1 Slice the rump steak into 8 thin slices and prepare each 'sandwich' as follows.

---

2 Place a slice of rump steak on a square of oiled foil, spread with cheese, a slice of ham, a layer of sliced mushrooms, another slice of ham, another layer of cheese, and top with a final slice of rump steak.

---

3 Season well and repeat the ingredients and layers for the other 3 'sandwiches'. Wrap each one loosely in the oiled foil and bake for 30 minutes.

---

4 Delicious as a hot snack, or as a main course served with baked potatoes and a green vegetable.

Rump Steaks with Gin and Juniper

Serves 4

This may sound like the ultimate in boozy recipes, but the alcohol content is driven off during the cooking process, so teetotallers may sit back and enjoy it.

4 rump steaks
2 dessert spoons crushed juniper
  berries
150ml/¼ pint double cream
2 tablespoons gin

Pre-heat oven to 190°C/375°F/Gas Mark 5.

---

1   Lay each steak on a square of oiled foil. Season well. Scatter over the juniper berries and pour an equal quantity of gin over each steak. Wrap loosely in foil parcels and cook for 30 minutes.

---

2   When ready to serve, open each parcel and drizzle a small amount of the cream through the opening.

---

3   The resultant sauce is so delicious you must serve a purée of potatoes or tagliatelli to soak it up for maximum effectiveness.

CHAPTER 6

GRILLING

Because venison is such a lean meat, care must be taken when grilling to keep the meat well basted or oiled. Pre-heat the grill on the maximum setting for at least a minute before starting to cook these recipes.

Basic Grilled Chops

Serves 4

4 loin chops, marinaded for a few
hours
dash of cooking oil
rowanberry or redcurrant jelly

1 Use the basic marinade for the chops, and season well.

2 Grill for about 5 minutes, brush with a little oil, then turn heat down and grill for about 10 minutes on each side, brushing with more oil half-way through cooking time.

3 Serve on hot plates with a purée of potato and a spoonful of rowanberry or redcurrant jelly.

Rump Steaks Dijonnaise

Serves 4

4 rump steaks
2 tablespoons Dijon mustard
1 dessert spoon brown sugar

1   Mix the sugar into the mustard and spread half the mixture over the steaks.

2   Grill for about 8–10 minutes. Turn over, spread with remaining mustard mixture and grill for a further 6–8 minutes.

3   This spicy topping can also be used on chops and grilled as in the previous recipe.

Fillet with Green Pepper Sauce

Serves 4

1 fillet (about 700g/1½lb)
basic marinade
25g/1oz butter
2 tablespoons green peppercorns
50g/2oz flour
275ml/½ pint milk

1 Cut the fillet into four pieces and marinade (overnight if possible – the sauce can also be made the night before if you are busy).

2 Melt the butter in a saucepan, add the flour, stir in the milk and thicken slowly to make a smooth roux sauce. Season well.

3 Crush half the green peppercorns and add to the sauce with the other whole peppercorns. Simmer gently for 10 minutes.

4 Meanwhile, grill the marinaded fillet steaks for about 5 minutes on each side.

5 Serve on hot plates and pour the sauce over the top. This dish is excellent served with pasta – tagliatelli is best, to coat and soak up the delicious sauce.

Venison Sausages with Apples

Serves 4

2–3 venison sausages per person
2 large cooking apples, peeled and
*   cored*
dash of cooking oil
25g/1oz butter
1 dessert spoon wine vinegar

1   Grill sausages for about 8–10 minutes on each side.

2   Meanwhile, put a little oil and the butter into a shallow pan. Slice the apples into thick slices and add to the pan. Fry gently for a few minutes and turn carefully.

3   Cook for another 5 minutes, turn up the heat and add the wine vinegar.

4   Dish the sausages and pour the apples with their spicy juices over the top.

5   Serve with rice and baked tomatoes.

Venison Sausages with Shell Pasta

Serves 4

This unusual recipe is popular with children and is easy for them to make too.

8 venison sausages
½ cucumber, peeled and cut into
  chunks
2 tablespoons fruit chutney
dash of cooking oil
225g/½lb shell pasta or wholewheat
  macaroni

1 Grill the venison sausages for about 8–10 minutes on each side.

2 Meanwhile gently fry the cucumber in the oil for a few minutes, stirring carefully. Turn off the heat and stir in the fruit chutney.

3 Cook the pasta as directed on the packet and drain well.

4 Serve the sausages on top of the pasta and pour over the sauce.

Cutlets with Chestnut Purée

Serves 2

This is a lovely recipe to cook for two in the cold winter months. It is very simple, but will not sit around too long, so if you suffer from 'late-mate syndrome', choose an alternative recipe from the casserole section.

2 double loin chops
1 small tin chestnut purée (for
    cheats), or
225g/8oz large chestnuts, cooked and
    puréed (for devotees) – in this case
    save 4 whole chestnuts for garnish
small quantity olive oil
salt and pepper
2 sprigs watercress to garnish

---

1 Brush chops with oil and season. Grill for 10 minutes on each side.

---

2 Spread chestnut purée on one side of each double chop and return to the grill for 5 minutes until bubbly and slightly brown.

---

3 Serve immediately, garnished with whole chestnuts and sprigs of watercress.

---

4 A baked selection of finely sliced root vegetables is best as an accompaniment.

Rump Steaks with Orange and Almonds

Serves 4

4 rump steaks
1 orange, thinly sliced
1 level dessert spoon sliced, blanched
  almonds
basic marinade plus juice of 1 orange

1 Marinade the steaks overnight, using extra orange juice.

2 Cook the steaks for 10 minutes on each side and place on an ovenproof serving dish.

3 Drizzle a small quantity of marinade over the steaks and top with sliced orange and sliced almonds.

4 Put back into warm oven for 10 minutes minimum – this would stretch to a ½ hour for guests who are late or who insist on another pre-dinner drink.

CHAPTER 7

FRYING

There are really only two cuts of venison suitable for frying – the fillet and the rump steak. We have included recipes for both, but also have included a delicious old fashioned patty, which is made from minced venison. When frying, we do recommend a light olive oil; it is more expensive than vegetable or corn oil, but the flavour is incomparable.

Venison Collops

Serves 4

This is a very early eighteenth-century recipe from Scotland. It is a rich and unusual combination of flavours. If you cannot get or cannot face the price of real oysters, then substitute plump mussels.

8 thin slices rump steak, beaten flat
grated rind of 1 lemon
25g/1oz dry breadcrumbs
50g/2oz fresh breadcrumbs
¼ teaspoon grated nutmeg
25g/1oz butter
275ml/½ pint game stock
8 large oysters, or
16 mussels
croûtons for garnish

1 Mix the breadcrumbs with the lemon rind, grated nutmeg and salt and pepper.

2 Dip the collops of venison in this mixture, covering both sides.

3 Melt the butter in a frying pan and fry the collops for about 10 minutes on each side until golden brown.

4 Meanwhile, simmer the stock with half the mussels or oysters for 5 minutes. Add fresh breadcrumbs to thicken the sauce and cook a further 5 minutes.

5 Serve the collops on a serving dish, garnished with the croûtons, and serve the sauce separately.

Fillet Steaks with Grapes and Brandy

Serves 4

This is a 'stun-your-friends' recipe, so only serve it to friends who are worthy of stunning – it is one of the more expensive dishes.

8 thin cut fillet steaks
225g/8oz green grapes, stoned and
  halved
150ml/¼ pint double cream
1 tablespoon cooking brandy
  (optional but almost essential)
1 tablespoon olive oil
25g/1oz butter

1 Melt the butter in the olive oil and stir-fry the steaks for 5 minutes on each side – they should be pink in the middle.

2 When your guests are actually sitting down, add the brandy, grapes and finally the cream. Stir through and serve immediately.

3 Serve with a purée of potato, garnished with chopped chives to soak up the delicious sauce. Follow with a plain green salad.

Rump Steaks with Red Cherries

Serves 4

4 rump steaks
1 tin pitted cherries with liquor
1 dessert spoon olive oil
25g/1oz arrowroot or cornflour
basic marinade
parsley or watercress to garnish

1 Use the basic marinade for the steaks overnight.

2 Fry in olive oil and butter for 10 minutes on each side, place on a serving dish and remove to a warm oven.

3 Add the thickening flour to the pan juices and stir well. Add the cherries and stir until you have a thick sauce – add a little water if it is too thick.

4 Serve the steaks with the thick coating of sauce and garnish with parsley or watercress.

Fillet with Dried Apricots

Serves 4

4 fillet steaks
50g/2oz unsalted butter
100g/4oz dried apricots, pre-soaked
  and cooked for 5 minutes
½ teaspoon brown sugar
2 tablespoons red wine vinegar
150ml/¼ pint game stock
watercress to garnish.

1 Melt the butter and sauté the venison steaks for about 5 minutes on each side. Remove from the heat and keep warm on a serving dish.

2 Add the sugar and red wine vinegar to the remaining butter and meat juices in the frying pan. Add the stock and cook for 5 minutes on high heat to reduce the sauce until it is quite thick and 'sticky'.

3 Add the apricots. When ready, pour the sauce over the steaks and garnish with watercress.

4 Serve with puréed potatoes or rice.

Venison Stroganoff

Serves 4

450g/1lb best fillet steak
225g/¹⁄₂lb button mushrooms
2 chopped leeks or
1 small chopped onion
275ml/¹⁄₂ pint sour cream or thick
   yoghurt
grated nutmeg
25g/1oz butter
1 teaspoon olive oil
1 teaspoon fresh chopped parsley to
   garnish

1 Slice the fillet steak into pieces about 2in/5cm × ¹⁄₂in/1cm thick. The dish is improved by the uniformity of the pieces, so abandon the sherry until later in the recipe for maximum concentration.

2 Melt the oil and butter in a heavy-based pan and add the chopped onion or leeks. Stir-fry gently for about 5 minutes.

3 Add the fillet steak and fry again for a further 10 minutes.

4 Take off the heat. Stir in the sour cream or yoghurt and garnish with a liberal grating of fresh nutmeg and the chopped parsley.

5 Serve on a bed of rice or tagliatelli.

Rump Steak with Savoury Lentils

Serves 4

Lentils cooked in this delicious way are a perfect accompaniment to fried rump steaks. You need only a green salad to complement the whole dish.

4 rump steaks
225g/½lb green or brown lentils,
    soaked for 1 hour
225g/½lb piece of salt pork or
    streaky bacon
1 clove crushed garlic
1 small onion, chopped
1 bouquet garni
1 dessert spoon of cooking oil
550ml/1 pint water
chopped parsley and grated lemon
    rind to garnish

1 In a heavy-based pan melt the oil. Add the chopped onion, drained lentils and the piece of salt pork or bacon. Stir-fry for about 5 minutes.

2 Add the water, garlic and bouquet garni. Bring to the boil and simmer for about 1 hour until the liquid has been absorbed and the lentils are quite tender.

3 Meanwhile fry the rump steaks for about 8 minutes on each side.

4 To serve, pour the lentils into a shallow serving dish, adjust the seasoning, cut the pork or bacon into strips and scatter over the top. Garnish with a little chopped parsley and grated lemon rind.

5 Serve a generous portion with each rump steak.

Fillet Mignon with Mustard Sauce

Serves 4

You can substitute stock or even water for the white wine or cognac in this recipe, but it is a bit of an insult to a prime fillet steak. Try to purloin some from somewhere, even if the guests miss one glass from their hors-d'oeuvre – it is well worth it.

4 fillet steaks, thickly cut
2 tablespoons chopped ham
1 teaspoon horseradish sauce
50g/2oz butter
1 finely chopped onion
1 bay leaf
pinch of thyme
juice of ½ lemon
1 tablespoon Dijon wholegrain
*   mustard*
150ml/¼ pint white wine or cognac

1   Season the steaks and set aside until the sauce is ready.

2   Melt the butter and gently fry the chopped onion and diced ham. Season with the thyme, bay leaf and horseradish sauce.

3   Stir in the white wine or cognac and simmer for 5 minutes, then stir in the Dijon mustard and a squeeze of fresh lemon. Keep warm.

4   Fry the fillet steaks in a little butter and oil until cooked to taste – about 5 minutes on each side for rare to medium-rare or 10 minutes for well done.

5   Serve the cooked steaks on a very hot plate and pour over this amazing sauce.

Venison Patties with Fried Egg and 'Mash'

Serves 4

450g/1lb minced venison
50g/2oz fresh white breadcrumbs
1 teaspoon thyme
1 large minced onion
1 teaspoon dried mustard
4 small eggs
oil for frying

---

1   Mix the venison, onion and seasoning in a mixing bowl. Form into 4 'patties' and coat with the fresh breadcrumbs.

---

2   Fry gently for about 10 minutes on each side. Remove from the heat and keep warm.

---

3   Break the eggs gently into the remaining fat and cook for about 4 minutes.

---

4   Top each venison patty with a fried egg and serve with mashed potato.

Venison Sausage with Fried Apple Rings

Serves 4

2–3 venison sausages per person
4 large apples – Bramley or Cox are
  best
50g/2oz butter

1 Peel and core the apples and cut into thick slices. Fry gently in the butter, turning carefully after 2–3 minutes. Remove and keep warm.

2 Meanwhile fry the sausages for about 10–15 minutes.

3 Serve the sausages on a bed of pasta or rice and top with the fried apple rings.

Hunters' Purses

Serves 4

This is a sumptuous dinner party recipe. Although the steaks have to be cooked at the last minute, the sauce and stuffing can be prepared the night before.

4 thick fillet steaks
1 glass of port – essential so do not
  skimp!
25g/1oz butter
sprigs of fresh rosemary, thyme and
  sage
50g/2oz game pâté, or a good liver
  pâté
150ml/¼ pint double cream
100g/4oz fresh cranberries or a small
  tin of cranberries

---

1 Marinade the steaks overnight in the port and chopped herbs. Remove from the marinade and drain well.

---

2 Simmer the cranberries with the marinade liquor until tender and then stir in the cream.

---

3 Fry the steaks in butter for about 5–8 minutes on each side.

---

4 Cut a pocket in the side of each steak and fill with the pâté.

---

5 Serve the filled steaks on a hot plate and pour over the cream and cranberry sauce.

CHAPTER 8

CASSEROLES

Of all the methods of cooking venison the casserole is probably the king. As venison has practically no fat, a slow casserole method will keep the meat and vegetables moist and succulent – and even better, the flavour will improve by cooking the day before. Casseroles freeze well and they can be up- or down-marketed with appropriate ingredients to suit your mood or your pocket. In short, it is the busy person's answer to producing cordon bleu cookery with the minimum amount of effort or sacrifice – which is how cooking should be.

Family Casserole

Serves 4–6

900g/2lb casserole venison in cubes –
  marinade overnight in basic
  marinade if possible
225g/8oz mushrooms, whole
1 large sliced onion
1 sliced green pepper
4 sliced carrots
2 sticks chopped celery
100g/4oz diced gammon or bacon
½ clove crushed garlic
25g/1oz flour
275ml/½ pint stock – a slosh of red
  wine also improves it

Pre-heat oven to 180°C/350°F/Gas Mark 4.

---

1 Stir-fry the vegetables in a little oil. Add the garlic, venison and bacon, stirring well. Add the flour and stock and stir again.

---

2 Transfer to a casserole dish, cover and cook for about 1½–2 hours until the meat is tender.

---

3 Serve with baked potatoes and a green salad.

Stuffed Shoulder with Ham and Herbs

Serves 4–6

Try to cook this in the summer months – the fresh herbs make all the difference.

1 boned fallow shoulder – smile
  sweetly at your butcher to achieve
  the boning
1 cupful cooked rice
150g/6oz chopped ham
1 dessert spoon fresh chopped thyme, or
1 pinch dried thyme
1 dessert spoon fresh parsley, or
1 pinch dried parsley
2 sprigs rosemary
2 sliced carrots
2 sliced celery sticks
1 sliced onion
150ml/¼ pint stock
salt and pepper

Pre-heat oven to 180°C/350°F/Gas Mark 4.

1 Combine the rice, ham and herbs. Season well.

2 Place in the cavity of the boned shoulder, roll up and tie in as neat a parcel as you can manage.

3 Put all the sliced vegetables in the bottom of a large casserole dish and moisten with stock.

4 Place the venison shoulder on this bed of vegetables and braise in a moderate oven for 2 hours.

5 Serve in thick slices with the vegetables as an accompaniment. The meat juices will saturate the bed of vegetables, giving a rich and aromatic depth of flavour – do not ruin it with gravy browning.

Stuffed Shoulder with Prunes

This is a richer alternative to the previous recipe. Substitute the ham with a stuffing of chopped prunes which have been soaked overnight in a little sherry or white wine. Cook the shoulder in the same way and use the remaining alcohol from the soaking to make a smooth, white béchamel sauce to serve with the slices of venison.

Shoulder Steaks with Cream and Mushrooms

Serves 4

4 shoulder steaks (about 225g/8oz
    each)
225g/½lb mushrooms
1 small onion, finely chopped
150ml/¼ pint single cream
150ml/¼ pint game stock
dash of cooking oil
25g/1oz flour
1 teaspoon chopped, fresh tarragon, or
¼ teaspoon dried tarragon, to
    garnish

Pre-heat oven to 180°C/350°F/Gas Mark 4.

---

1 Seal the steaks by frying quickly in a little oil. Transfer to a casserole dish and add the onion and mushrooms.

---

2 Stir the flour into the remaining oil and meat juices, and add the game stock. Heat through slowly until it thickens.

---

3 Pour over the steaks and vegetables and cook for 1 hour in a slow oven.

---

4 When ready to serve, pour over the cream and garnish with the tarragon.

Rich Venison Casserole with Herb Dumplings

Serves 4

450–700g/1–1½lb best casserole
 venison
1 medium onion, sliced
2 carrots, sliced
2 sticks celery, chopped
1 green pepper, sliced
1 small orange
150ml/¼ pint red wine
2 cloves
pinch of grated nutmeg
25g/1oz flour
dash of cooking oil

For the dumplings:
100g/4oz plain flour
1 teaspoon baking powder
50g/2oz butter or margarine
1 teaspoon dried mixed herbs
dash of milk

Pre-heat oven to 180°C/350°F/Gas Mark 4.

---

1 Gently fry the venison, onion, carrot, celery and green pepper in a little oil for about 5 minutes.

---

2 Stir in the flour to coat the mixture, then add the red wine and the orange juice.

---

3 Simmer gently for another 5 minutes and then transfer to a casserole dish. Put in the cloves and nutmeg and season to taste. Cook in oven for 1 hour.

---

4 Meanwhile make the dumplings. Rub the fat into the plain flour and baking powder. Add the mixed herbs. Use the milk to form a dryish dough. Form into about 8 small dumplings.

---

5 After the casserole has been cooked for 1 hour, put the dumplings on top of the meat and vegetables and return to the oven for a further 20 minutes.

Pot Roast with Lentils

Serves 4–6

Lentils are a lovely complement to venison. They absorb the meat juices to enhance the flavour and even better, they stretch a meal to accommodate extra hungry, unexpected guests.

1 boned, rolled fallow shoulder
225g/½lb green or brown lentils
1 small onion, chopped
2 small carrots, thinly sliced
1 clove garlic
275ml/½ pint game stock or water
1 large tin of tomatoes

Pre-heat oven to 180°C/350°F/Gas Mark 4.

---

1 Bring the game stock to the boil in a large saucepan. Add the lentils, vegetables, tomatoes and garlic and simmer, stirring occasionally, for 20 minutes.

---

2 Transfer to a casserole dish. Put the venison joint on top of this mixture and cook in a slow to moderate oven for about 1½ hours.

---

3 Serve a spoonful of the lentil mixture with a thick slice of the venison – no dainty slices here.

Pot Roast with Roebuck Sauce

Serves 4

This has an old English sauce with a piquant flavour.

1 boned fallow shoulder, or
1 small boned haunch
275ml/½ pint game stock
1 onion, finely chopped
100g/4oz chopped ham
½ cup wine vinegar
sprig parsley
pinch thyme
1 bay leaf
1 tablespoon redcurrant jelly
1 teaspoon cornflour or arrowroot
knob of butter

Pre-heat oven to 190°C/375°F/Gas Mark 5.

---

1   Place the venison in a casserole dish, pour over the game stock and cook in a moderate oven for about 1 hour.

---

2   Meanwhile make the sauce. Gently fry the onion and ham in a little butter until golden. Add the herbs and wine vinegar, turn the heat up and reduce the mixture by about half.

---

3   Remove from the heat, add the redcurrant jelly and stir in the cornflour. Simmer the sauce for a further 10 minutes.

---

4   When the meat is done, remove from the oven and cut into thick slices. Use the remaining stock to thin down the sauce if necessary and pour over the meat.

---

5   Serve with baked potatoes and a green vegetable.

Cassoulet

Serves 6–8

This is an updated and much less calorific variation of those well remembered traditional Languedoc cassoulets which need a follow-up of indigestion tablets in the middle of the night! Its combination of flavours makes it unusual enough for a dinner party, but you can make it with more humble leftovers for a family meal. This recipe may sound complicated, but it can be prepared the night before up to the last 1½-hours' cooking stage.

This particular variation is dedicated to a friend of ours, Nancy North. She compiled the dish with us on a memorable holiday in France over an equally memorable cassoulet and many glasses of claret.

For the haricot mixture:
225g/½lb haricot beans, soaked overnight
225g/½lb piece of belly of pork
1 onion, studded with four cloves
1 carrot
2 garlic cloves, crushed

For the meat mixture:
450g/1lb cubed shoulder or haunch
225g/½lb diced boneless chicken or turkey
4–6 pork sausages
bouquet garni
275ml/½ pint game stock
1 tablespoon tomato purée

Pre-heat oven to 180°C/350°F/Gas Mark 4.

1 Combine the haricot mixture ingredients. Add enough water to just cover the beans. Simmer for 1 hour.

2 Meanwhile, in a different pan, simmer all the ingredients of the meat mixture, also for 1 hour.

3 Then, the interesting bit. In a large casserole dish, alternate layers of the bean and meat mixture, seasoning well. Remove the bouquet garni before some unfortunate guest gets a forkful.

4 Cook in a slow oven for a further 1½ hours before serving.

Rump Steaks with Apricots and Prunes

Serves 4

4 rump steaks
12 stoned prunes
12 dried apricots, soaked overnight
275ml/½ pint chicken or game stock
1 tablespoon red wine vinegar
pinch of cinnamon
25g/1oz butter
25g/1oz flour

Pre-heat oven to 190°C/375°F/Gas Mark 5.

1   Gently fry the steaks in the butter and transfer to a casserole.

2   Stir the flour into the remaining butter, add the wine vinegar, cinnamon and stock and simmer for 5 minutes until thick.

3   Pour this sauce over the steaks, add the dried fruit and season to taste.

4   Cook for 1 hour in a moderate oven.

Boned Shoulder with Cranberries

Serves 4

1 boned fallow shoulder, marinaded
*   overnight*
225g/½lb fresh, cooked cranberries
*   or 1 small tin of cranberries if you*
*   are in a hurry*
150ml/¼ pint game stock
1 small chopped onion
1 small chopped carrot
1 stick celery, finely chopped
1 clove garlic, crushed

Pre-heat oven to 180°C/350°F/Gas Mark 4.

---

1 Braise the venison in a slow oven on the vegetables and moistened with stock for about 1 hour.

---

2 Pour over the cranberries and cook for a further 20 minutes.

---

3 Serve in thick wedges with the sauce poured over, and with puréed potatoes and a green salad.

Casserole Provençale

Serves 4–6

900g/2lb best casserole venison
1 sliced onion
2 sliced carrots
12–16 black olives
1 large tin of tomatoes
225g/½lb mushrooms, whole
2 cloves garlic, crushed
275ml/½ pint game or chicken stock
dash of cooking oil

Pre-heat oven to 180°C/350°F/Gas Mark 4.

---

1 Gently fry the venison, onion and carrots along with the garlic in a little cooking oil. Transfer to a casserole dish.

---

2 Add the whole mushrooms, olives and the tomatoes with the stock and stir well. Cook for approximately 1½ hours until the meat is tender.

---

3 Serve with hunks of French bread and a green salad.

Shoulder with Red Cabbage

Serves 4

1 shoulder – fallow if possible
1 large sliced onion
1 large sliced cooking apple
4 cloves
1 clove garlic, crushed
150ml/¼ pint wine vinegar
1 small red cabbage, roughly sliced
dash of cooking oil
ground black pepper

Pre-heat oven to 180°C/350°F/Gas Mark 4.

1 Gently fry the cabbage in a little cooking oil. Add the onion, apple, cloves and garlic, stirring well.

2 Transfer to a casserole dish and pour over the red wine vinegar. Season with ground black pepper.

3 Top this mixture with the shoulder of venison and cook in a slow oven for about 1½ hours.

4 This is good when served with rice or noodles.

Boned Haunch with Ratatouille

Serves 4–6

This recipe was given to us by Mary Glenister, with whom we have shared many gastronomic delights over the years.

1 boneless haunch, marinaded
  overnight
2 green peppers, thickly sliced
3 courgettes, thickly sliced
1 large aubergine, sliced
1 medium onion, sliced
1 large tin of tomatoes
2 cloves garlic, crushed
1 tablespoon olive oil

Pre-heat oven to 190°C/375°F/Gas Mark 5.

---

1 Fry the fresh vegetables in the oil with the garlic for about 10 minutes, stirring well. Transfer to a casserole dish, pour over the tomatoes, lay the venison joint on top and season well.

---

2 Cook in a moderate oven, for about 1½ hours.

---

3 Serve with baked potatoes.

Steak and Kidney Pie

Serves 4

450g/1lb best casserole venison
225g/½lb venison kidney
1 sliced onion
2 sliced carrots
150ml/¼ pint game stock
1 tablespoon tomato purée
225g/½lb flaky pastry (ready-made
  shop pastry will do very well)
dash of cooking oil
1 bay leaf
pinch of thyme

Pre-heat oven to 190°C/375°F/Gas Mark 5.

---

1 Fry the casserole venison, kidney, onion and carrots in a little oil. Add the herbs, tomato purée and game stock.

---

2 Transfer to a deep casserole or pie dish and cook for about 1 hour.

---

3 Meanwhile, roll out the pastry and prepare a decoration of 6 pastry leaves for garnish.

---

4 When the meat is cooked, put the pastry 'lid' on top, garnish with pastry leaves and return to oven for a further ½ hour.

Braised Haunch with Juniper and Sour Cream

Serves 4–6

1 boneless haunch, marinaded
  overnight
1 chopped onion
2 chopped carrots
1 stick chopped celery
1 chopped turnip
2 cloves crushed garlic
150ml/¼ pint game stock
25g/1oz juniper berries
275ml/½ pint sour cream

Pre-heat oven to 190°C/375°F/Gas Mark 5.

1   Braise the venison with half of the crushed juniper berries on a bed of the vegetables and garlic, moistened with the game stock for about 1½ hours.

2   When ready to serve, slice into thick slices, pour over the sour cream, slightly warmed and scatter over the remaining crushed juniper berries.

3   Delicious served with tagliatelli to soak up the sauce.

Sausage and Kidney Casserole

Serves 4

This is an easy recipe to assemble from store cupboard ingredients.

8 venison sausages
8 small venison kidneys, preferably
  from the roe deer
1 large tin of tomatoes
1 dessert spoon of soy sauce
1 small chopped onion
pinch dried oregano
bay leaf
dash of oil
25g/1oz flour

Pre-heat oven to 190°C/375°F/Gas Mark 5.

---

1 Fry the sausages, kidneys and onion in a little oil for about 2–3 minutes.

---

2 Add the flour and stir through. Pour over the tin of tomatoes and soy sauce and stir again.

---

3 Transfer to a casserole dish, add the herbs and cook for about 1 hour.

---

4 Serve with savoury rice or spaghetti.

Spicy Venison with Yoghurt and Cucumber

Serves 4

500g/1¼lb best casserole venison
2 chopped leeks
100g/¼lb button mushrooms
1 red pepper, thickly sliced
150ml/¼ pint thick yoghurt
½ cucumber, peeled and cut into 1in/
*   2½cm chunks*
1 clove garlic
150ml/¼ pint game or chicken stock
dash of cooking oil

Pre-heat oven to 190°C/375°F/Gas Mark 5.

---

1 Gently fry the venison, leeks, mushrooms and pepper in a little cooking oil for about 5 minutes.

---

2 Transfer to a casserole dish, add the crushed garlic and pour over the stock. Cook for 1 hour in a moderate oven.

---

3 Add the cucumber chunks and cook for a further 15 minutes.

---

4 When ready to serve, pour over the yoghurt and serve immediately on portions of rice.

CHAPTER 9

VENISON IN THE
SLOW-COOKER

We have no microwave in our kitchen but would not be without a slow-cooker. This first recipe is a traditional steamed pudding, which is perfectly adapted to a slow-cooker. It can be cooked overnight without turning the kitchen into a Turkish bath.

Steamed Venison Pudding

Serves 4–6

700g/1½lb cubed, casserole venison
100g/4oz sliced mushrooms
1 small chopped onion
pinch mixed herbs
salt and pepper
150ml/¼pint rich stock

For the suet crust:
225g/8oz plain flour
100g/4oz shredded suet or margarine
½ teaspoon baking powder
1 tablespoon milk

1 Make suet crust by rubbing the suet into the flour. Add baking powder and bind with milk.

2 Roll out the crust and line a 2-pint pudding basin with it, saving a round of pastry for the lid.

3 Heat the stock in a saucepan, add the meat and vegetables and season well.

4 Place the mixture in the pastry-lined basin and top with a pastry lid, sealing it well with watered fingertips.

5 Place in water in slow-cooker for 4 hours on a high setting or overnight for 8 hours on 'low'.

Casserole with Tomatoes and Rosemary

Serves 4–6

Cook this recipe in late summer when fresh tomatoes are cheap and plentiful.

700g/1½lb casserole venison, thickly
*   cut*
1 medium onion or 2 leeks, finely
*   chopped*
25g/1oz wholemeal breadcrumbs
450g/1lb fresh tomatoes, skinned by
*   immersing in boiling water for 10*
*   minutes*
sprig of fresh rosemary
150ml/¼ pint game stock
dash of cooking oil
150ml/¼ pint thick yoghurt

Pre-heat slow-cooker on 'high' for ½ an hour.

1   Fry the venison and onion or leeks in a litle oil for about 5 minutes. Transfer to the slow-cooker.

2   Add the tomatoes, rosemary and pour over the stock. Season well.

3   Cook as directed on your slow-cooker for about 4 hours on 'high' setting.

4   Switch to 'slow' setting, add the breadcrumbs and cook for a further 1 hour. The crumbs thicken the sauce giving it a lovely 'body' without using more fat or flour.

5   When ready to serve, pour over the yoghurt and serve with rice or pasta and a plain green salad.

Mixed Game Roast

Serves 4–6

Any of the small roasting joints may be roasted in the slow-cooker – small cuts of rump steak, boned haunch or fillet are the best. This recipe uses venison and game for a most unusual combination of flavours. We have included liver and kidney, but these can be omitted if you do not care for offal.

1 dessert spoon olive oil
2 garlic cloves, crushed or sliced
2 rashers smoked bacon cut into
*   pieces*
sprig fresh sage or thyme

Plus choose any of the following:
4–6 rump steaks or fillets
6 small loin chops
100g/¼lb thinly sliced liver
4–6 kidneys, cut in half
4 pigeon breasts
4 pheasant breasts or thighs
4 rabbit pieces – saddle or leg

Pre-heat slow-cooker on 'high' for ½ an hour.

1 Put the olive oil, garlic, bacon and herbs into the slow-cooker. Add your chosen selection of venison and game pieces and stir into the oil and garlic.

2 Cook on 'high' for 4 hours, then reduce to the 'low' setting for a further 1 hour.

3 Serve with roast or baked potatoes and a selection of root vegetables – celeriac is particularly good.

Venison Goulash

Serves 4–6

700g/1½lb best casserole venison,
  cubed
3 carrots, thickly sliced
2 onions, thickly sliced
1 medium turnip, diced
1 clove garlic, crushed
small tin of tomato purée
2 tablespoons paprika
1 bay leaf
pinch dried thyme
150ml/¼ pint game stock
dash of cooking oil

Pre-heat slow-cooker on 'high' for ½ an hour.

1   Heat the cooking oil in a saucepan and add the root vegetables and venison. Cook for about 5 minutes, stirring frequently. Add the garlic, tomato purée, paprika and herbs.

2   Transfer to the slow-cooker and pour over the game stock. Cook for 4–6 hours on the 'low' setting.

Carbonnade with Mustard Dumplings

Serves 4–6

700g/1½lb diced casserole venison
50g/2oz demerara sugar
1 tablespoon black treacle
550ml/1 pint beer, or
275ml/½ pint beer and 275ml/½
*   pint water*

For the dumplings:
100g/4oz plain flour
1 teaspoon baking powder
50g/2oz margarine
1 dessert spoon dry mustard
dash of milk

Pre-heat slow-cooker on 'high' for ½ an hour.

1   Dissolve the sugar and treacle in the beer and bring gently to the boil. Put the venison in the slow cooker and pour over the boiling liquid. Cook on the 'low' setting for 4 hours.

2   Meanwhile make the dumplings. Rub the margarine into the flour and baking powder until it resembles fine breadcrumbs. Add the dry mustard and mix with the milk to form a smooth dough.

3   Form 6–8 small dumplings and put these onto the meat mixture after it has cooked for 4 hours.

4   Reset the control to 'high' and cook for a further 1 hour to finish the dumplings.

5   Serve with plenty of vegetables and a purée of potatoes to soak up the marvellous sauce.

CHAPTER 10

THE COLD BUFFET

Venison can form the basis of excellent cold dishes, and there are many variations of pâtés, pies and terrines. Many of these are highly complicated and strike a note of terror with visions of slaving in the kitchen for hours, chopping, mixing and layering. We believe strongly in the fun of cooking, so the following recipes can be adapted to your mood.

If you are busy, the family cantankerous, then forget the pâté and terrine and settle for sausages and pasta salad. But if you feel peaceful and creative and there is a good programme on the radio, then choose a pâté or game pie, pour yourself a glass of wine for company – and enjoy yourself.

Meat Loaf with Rowanberry Glaze

Serves 4–6

This recipe can also be made in a ring mould which always looks more impressive. When turned out, the ring can be filled with a mixture of sliced mushrooms and watercress in a French dressing. This is a lovely dish for a warm summer evening.

450g/1lb casserole venison, minced
1 onion, minced
100g/4oz cooked ham, minced
2 tomatoes, finely chopped
2 heaped tablespoons breadcrumbs
1 beaten egg
1 teaspoon grated lemon rind
¼ teaspoon grated nutmeg
salt and pepper
2 tablespoons rowanberry or
 redcurrant jelly

1 Combine the first 5 ingredients and mix well. Add the lemon rind and nutmeg and season. Add the beaten egg and stir again.

2 Press the mixture into a foil-lined loaf tin and cook in a medium oven for about 1 hour.

3 Allow to cool. Turn out on to wire rack and spread all over with rowanberry or redcurrant jelly.

4 Leave overnight before slicing.

Spiced Venison

Serves 8–10

This takes a little more time and organisation – in other words you must start it a week before you eat it! But it is so worth the effort, that you will repeat the recipe many times. It is especially nice on Boxing Day when the hangovers will not stand even a whiff of more turkey.

1 boneless haunch, rolled and tied
2 tablespoons salt
15g/1/2oz allspice
1 teaspoon ground ginger
15g/1/2oz ground black pepper
1 teaspoon grated nutmeg
1 teaspoon ground cloves
100g/4oz brown sugar – soft brown
  sugar is best
4 carrots
1/2 swede or turnip
2 large sliced potatoes

1 Place the venison in a large glass or earthenware bowl. Rub all over with the salt, spices and sugar.

2 Turn it every day and baste with the liquid forming at the bottom of the bowl.

3 After 5 days take the meat out, wash thoroughly and place in large saucepan. Cover with cold water and the remaining spicy marinade.

4 Bring slowly to the boil, add the vegetables and cook for 2–5 hours until tender.

5 Cool in the liquid and refrigerate overnight before slicing.

Venison Pie

Serves 6–8

900g/2lb casserole venison, finely
    diced
100g/¼ lb venison liver, thinly sliced
100g/¼lb cooked, smoked ham,
    diced
1 large onion, finely chopped
2 carrots, finely chopped
1 stick celery, finely chopped
1 teaspoon crushed juniper berries
1 dessert spoon chopped, fresh parsley
pinch grated nutmeg
150ml/¼ pint game stock
dash of cooking oil
1 clove garlic
beaten egg or milk to glaze

For the pastry:
150g/6oz plain flour
75g/3oz butter or margarine
water to mix

Pre-heat oven to 190°C/375°F/Gas Mark 5.

---

1   Heat the oil in a heavy-based saucepan. Add the venison, liver, vegetables
    and crushed garlic clove. Stir frequently and cook for about 5 minutes.

---

2   Transfer half the mixture to a deep pie dish and season well. Sprinkle on half
    of the chopped ham, then another layer of meat and vegetable mixture. Top
    with the last of the ham and scatter the juniper berries on top. Add the port,
    stock, parsley and nutmeg.

---

3   Cook in a slow oven for about 1½ hours until the meats are tender.

---

4   Meanwhile make the pastry. Rub the fat into the flour and form into a dough
    with a little water. Roll out until about ½cm/¼in thick.

---

5   Remove the pie dish from the oven and let it cool slightly. (Alternatively, the
    stages up until this point may be done the day before.)

6 Put the pastry over the meat mixture and decorate with pastry 'leaves' and 'flowers' if you feel inspired. brush the whole pastry lid with beaten egg or milk and return to the oven to cook for a further 30 minutes until golden brown. Be sure to make at least two vent holes in the pastry lid.

Venison and Game Pie

This is a variation on the previous recipe. To the basic venison meat mixture, you can add any of the following game: hare; rabbit; pheasant; partridge; mallow; teal; or pigeon. The joints must be boneless, but it is a good way of using up bits of game, especially if you have a good source of game birds – like a spouse or friend who shoots, for example.

Venison Liver Pâté

Serves 4–6

This simple but delicious dish was given to us by Angela Roffey at whose generous and expansive dinner table we tasted our first venison dish.

1 roe liver – about 450g/1lb, chopped
1 large onion, finely chopped
6 rashers streaky bacon, chopped
pinch mixed herbs
1 small glass sherry
1 clove garlic, crushed
single cream (optional)

1 Fry the bacon and onion in the butter until soft. Add the chopped liver and stir-fry for a few minutes.

2 Remove from the pan and put into a liquidiser together with the herbs, garlic, black pepper and sherry. Liquidise until smooth. If the mixture is too thick, then add a little more sherry or some single cream.

3 Pour into individual ramekin dishes and chill until firm.

Game Terrine

Serves 6–8

450g/1lb roe or fallow liver, diced
1 pheasant, boned and diced
1 rabbit, boned and diced
225g/½lb streaky pork, diced
2 eggs, beaten thoroughly
1 clove garlic, crushed
1 tablespoon fresh chopped thyme, or
pinch dried thyme
1 crumbled bay leaf
pinch grated nutmeg
1 tablespoon brandy

Pre-heat oven to 190°C/375°F/Gas Mark 5.

1 Mix all the ingredients in a large mixing bowl until thoroughly combined. Season well and pack into a terrine dish.

2 Cook in a medium oven for about 2 hours. Test the terrine by piercing with a skewer. If the juices run clear then it is done.

3 Remove from the heat and if possible put a weight on the top.

4 Refrigerate overnight before serving.

Layered Game and Liver Terrine

Serves 6–8

This recipe is a more complicated and certainly more expensive one, but it is well worth the time and money! It freezes well and as it is quite rich, a small portion will suffice even the hungriest of guests.

450g/1lb fillet, thinly sliced
225g/½lb roe liver, thinly sliced
1 pheasant, boned and diced
225g/½lb belly pork, chopped
225g/½lb pork sausage meat
100g/4oz mushrooms, open or field if
   possible, sliced
1 medium onion, finely chopped
1 carrot, thinly sliced
1 pinch grated nutmeg
1 tablespoon olive oil
1 cup red wine
1 sprig thyme
2 sprigs parsley
1 bay leaf
2 cloves garlic, crushed

Pre-heat oven to 180°C/350°F/Gas Mark 4.

1 Put the pheasant, venison fillet, liver and the belly of pork into a large mixing bowl. Add the mushrooms, onion, carrots, garlic, herbs and nutmeg. Season well and pour over the red wine and oil. Leave to marinade overnight, or even over two nights – it will improve with keeping.

2 When ready for cooking, line a large terrine with the sausage meat. Layer the meats one at a time, together with the sliced vegetables as they come. Strain the marinade and pour over the layered meats.

3 Cover with a piece of oiled foil and cook in a slow oven for 2–3 hours. Remove from the heat, put a weight on top and refrigerate for at least 24 hours before serving.

These three preceding recipes are just a cross-section of the many variations that you can produce from a venison and game mixture. Be adventurous. If you have spent the housekeeping money on a 'Gucci' handbag or a set of golf clubs, then plump for the liver pâté. But if you are confined to the house with flu, and have not spent money for days, then go for the game and liver terrine. You may substitute wild duck, partridge, pigeon or even grouse for the game ingredients listed.

Sausage and Pasta Salad

Serves 4–6

This recipe has appeared in a different form earlier in the book, but this cold version is sensational and very simple. The kids will love it, and you can vary the ingredients according to what you have left over in the fridge.

450g/1lb venison sausages
2 leeks, finely sliced
225g/½lb button mushrooms
1 green pepper, finely sliced
dash of cooking oil
1 clove garlic, crushed
225g/½lb shell pasta
1 pinch dried oregano
2 tablespoons good mayonnaise

1 Cook the pasta as directed until al dente, season well and leave to cool, scattering the oregano over the mixture.

2 Grill the venison sausages for about 8 minutes on each side.

3 Meanwhile fry the leek, pepper and mushrooms for about 5 minutes in a little cooking oil and garlic. (All this preparation can be done the day before.)

4 When ready to assemble, put the pasta into a mixing bowl, and the cooled sausages, cut into small pieces and stir well. Add the fried vegetable mixture and again stir well to mix in all the flavours. Check the seasoning again. Lastly, fold in the mayonnaise and chill the mixture for at least 2 hours.

5 Serve on a bed of lettuce as part of a cold buffet, or with cold savoury rice and a green salad as a main course.

Cold Sliced Venison with Piquant Dressing

Serves 6–8

This is a lovely dish to present in high summer when you can get fresh herbs.

1 joint, boneless haunch or fillet
150ml/¼ pint mayonnaise
1 dessert spoon chopped gherkins
1 tablespoon chopped cucumber
1 tablespoon chopped red peppers
1 tablespoon chopped anchovies
1 teaspoon fresh chopped parsley
1 teaspoon fresh chopped chives
1 teaspoon fresh chopped lemon balm
fresh parsley and mint sprigs to
    garnish.

1   Roast the venison in foil the day before and leave to cool in the foil wrapping.

2   Combine the rest of the ingredients in a large mixing bowl and season to taste.

3   When ready to serve, slice the venison on a long serving dish and pour over the piquant sauce.

4   Serve with rice and garnish with fresh parsley and mint sprigs.

Venison and Mushroom Ring Mould

Serves 6–8

1½kg/3lb boneless haunch
1 small onion, finely chopped
100g/¼lb mushrooms, sliced
4 tomatoes, skinned and chopped
100g/4oz cucumber, chopped
1 teaspoon fresh, chopped thyme, or
pinch of dried thyme
275ml/½ pint aspic
dash of cooking oil
1 clove garlic, crushed
sliced mushrooms and sliced
*   tomatoes, or watercress to garnish*

1 Roast the venison in foil the day before. Set aside to cool and then cut into small pieces. Season well.

2 Meanwhile, fry the vegetables in the cooking oil and garlic until soft – about 5–8 minutes, stirring well. Set aside to cool.

3 Make up the aspic as directed. Oil a ring mould with cooking oil.

4 Combine the vegetable mixture and venison and put into the ring mould. Pour over the aspic and refrigerate overnight, or for at least 3 hours.

5 When ready to serve, unmould the ring carefully onto a plate or a cold rice salad.

6 Fill the centre with sliced mushrooms, sliced tomatoes or just a few sprigs of watercress.

Cold Roast Venison with Fruit Compote

Serves 6–8

This is a perfect recipe for 'night-before' cooking. Prepare and roast the meat in advance and also prepare the compote the day before. The flavours improve with keeping overnight.

For the roast meat:
1 boneless haunch (1½–2kg/3–4lb)
spicy marinade

For the fruit compote:
100g/4oz pitted prunes, soaked
    overnight
100g/4oz dried apricots, soaked
    overnight
1 fresh orange, cut into four pieces
1 tablespoon wine vinegar
1 tablespoon rowanberry or
    redcurrant jelly
4 pickled gherkins, sliced
ground black pepper

1   Marinade the venison overnight in the spicy marinade – *see* Chapter 2, then roast it in a medium oven for about 1½ hours using the foil method. Leave to cool in the foil.

2   Meanwhile make the fruit compote. Combine the fruit in a small saucepan, add the red wine vinegar and simmer slowly for 30 minutes.

3   Add the gherkins and rowanberry or redcurrant jelly and cook for a further 10 minutes. Season with black pepper and leave to cool.

4   When ready to assemble, slice the cold roast venison and arrange on a serving dish. Pour over the fruit compote mixture and refrigerate before serving. Alternatively, serve the compote separately in a sauce boat.

CHAPTER 11

OFFAL

Offal always seems a rather degrading name for such delicious by-
products, and if you ever get the chance to sample venison liver and
kidneys, then grab it at once. They are usually the stalker's perks, but are
much prized – especially when from the roe deer.

Fried Liver with Sage Leaves and Mushrooms

Serves 4

1 roe liver, thinly sliced
8–10 fresh sage leaves
225g/8oz sliced mushrooms
salt and pepper
1 teaspoon dry mustard powder
1 dessert spoon olive oil
25g/1oz butter

1 Heat the oil and butter in a pan, add the sliced liver and stir-fry quite quickly for about 3 minutes – the liver should remain pink inside.

2 Add the sage leaves, mustard, mushrooms and seasoning, turn the heat down and cook for a further 5 minutes, stirring well.

3 Serve immediately.

Brochettes of Kidney

Serves 4

Try very hard to prise tender roe kidneys from the breakfast pan of the stalker. If unsuccessful, use thick sliced fallow or red deer kidneys.

12 roe kidneys, or
12 thick slices fallow kidney
basic or spicy marinade
4 rolls streaky bacon
8 mushrooms
1 large onion, quartered
4 sprigs fresh rosemary

1 Turn the kidneys in the marinade overnight or for 2–10 hours.

2 Thread onto skewers, alternating with the next four ingredients.

3 Grill on each side, brushing with the remaining marinade.

4 Serve on a bed or rice with chopped tomatoes and garnish with a sprig of rosemary.

Baked Whole Liver with Sage and Bacon

Serves 4

This is one of the most delicious and unusual recipes for cooking liver. It is essential to use the liver from the roe deer as it has a much finer texture than the coarser fallow liver.

1 whole roe liver
8 fresh sage leaves
8 very thin rashers of streaky bacon,
  de-rinded

For the tomato sauce:
1 large tin of peeled plum tomatoes
1 teaspoon Worcester sauce
½ clove crushed garlic
½ chopped onion
dash of cooking oil

Pre-heat oven to 200°C/400°F/Gas Mark 6.

1 On a chopping board, spread the rashers of bacon side by side. Lay the sage leaves on the bacon, also side by side.

2 Finally put the whole liver onto the middle of the bacon slices, season well and bring the bacon rashers up over the liver, until the whole liver is covered with bacon and sage leaves.

3 Wrap the whole lot in oiled foil and bake in the oven for 20 minutes if you like your liver pink, or 30 minutes for more well-cooked liver.

4 Meanwhile make the sauce. Gently fry the onion and garlic in a little cooking oil. Add the tin of tomatoes and Worcester sauce, season well and simmer gently with a lid over until you have a thick tomato sauce. It will take about 15 minutes, stirring occasionally.

5 To serve, slice the liver with a sharp knife in thin diagonal slices and pour over the tomato sauce. It is delicious served on a bed of rice or pasta.

Stuffed Hearts

Serves 4

4 roe hearts, trimmed
50g/2oz cooked rice
50g/2oz sultanas
1 apple, peeled, cored and chopped
1 stick celery, finely chopped
pinch dried thyme, or
two sprigs fresh thyme
grated rind of ½ a lemon
275ml/½ pint game stock

Pre-heat oven to 180°C/350°F/Gas Mark 4.

---

1 Combine the rice, sultanas, apple, celery, thyme and lemon rind. Season well and use this stuffing to fill the cavities of each heart.

---

2 Heat the game stock and pour into a small casserole dish. Arrange the stuffed hearts in this stock, so that they stand up on end – do not choose a casserole that is too wide.

---

3 Cook in a slow to moderate oven for about 1½ hours.

---

4 If required, you can thicken the gravy with a little beurre manie or a dessert spoon of cornflour. Thin or thick, serve the hearts with mashed potato to soak up the rich juices. This is also good when cooked in the slow cooker.

Fried Kidneys with Vermouth and Cream

Serves 4

This is one of the few recipes in the book which is not low in calories, but it is so delicious that you must not miss out on it. An extra brisk walk the next day will take care of the cream and butter, but do not use a substitute – butter is best!

8 roe kidneys, cut in half
2 tablespoons dry vermouth
150ml/¼ pint single cream
25g/1oz butter

1 Melt the butter in a pan and gently fry the kidneys, stirring frequently so that the butter does not burn.

2 When they are cooked, add the vermouth, turn up the heat and cook fiercely for about ½ a minute.

3 Turn off the heat, add the cream, stir quickly and serve right away on a bed of rice with a plain green salad.

Chinese Style Liver with Noodles

Serves 4

450g/1lb sliced venison liver, roe if
*   possible*
1 small onion, finely chopped
100g/4oz sliced mushrooms
1 teaspoon tomato purée
1 tablespoon soy sauce
a little fresh grated ginger, if liked
100g/4oz beansprouts
dash of cooking oil
225g/8oz noodles or tagliatelli
fresh parsley to garnish

---

1 Heat the cooking oil in a shallow pan and gently fry the onion until soft but not coloured.

---

2 Meanwhile cut the liver slices into small strips. Add to the oil and onion, turn up the heat and fry quickly for about 3 minutes, stirring occasionally.

---

3 Add the mushrooms, beansprouts, tomato purée and soy sauce.

---

4 Turn the heat down again, and continue to cook for a further 5 minutes, adding a little water if necessary. Finally add the grated ginger.

---

5 Cook the noodles or tagliatelli as directed and drain well.

---

6 Serve the liver mixture heaped on the noodles and garnish with fresh parsley.

Venison Liver Casserole

Serves 4

450g/1lb roe or fallow liver, sliced
1 onion, sliced
1 stick of celery, sliced
2 carrots, sliced
bouquet garni
25g/1oz flour
25g/½ pint game or meat stock
dash of cooking oil

Pre-heat oven to 190°C/375°F/Gas mark 5.

1 Fry the liver in the oil for about 1 minute on each side to seal the juices. Transfer to a casserole dish.

2 Add the sliced vegetables and the bouquet garni and season well.

3 Stir the flour into the remaining oil, add the stock and simmer until thickened, stirring well. Pour this over the liver and vegetables and cook in a slow oven for just over 1 hour.

CHAPTER 12

LEFTOVERS

Provided you have not overcooked the meat, a joint of cold, roast venison is very good sliced up and served with puréed potatoes or baked potatoes and salad. But if you have a quantity of left-over meat and the family is in revolt against another day of cold cuts, then try some of these unusual ways of using up the leftovers.

Potted Venison with Nutmeg

Serves 4

This is an old Elizabethan recipe using cold, cooked venison.

450g/1lb cooked venison, minced,
1 small chopped onion,
1 teaspoon finely chopped thyme
1/2 teaspoon grated nutmeg
1/4 teaspoon finely grated orange peel
small quantity cold meat stock,
*   jellied if possible*
salad to garish

1 Combine all the ingredients, seasoning well. Add the stock to moisten the mixture and press into individual small dishes or one big dish. Put a weight on top and leave overnight.

2 When ready to serve, unmould the potted venison onto a plate, and garnish with salad.

3 This is very good served with a cold rice and tomato salad.

Shepherds' Pie with Ham

Serves 4

350g/³/₄lb cold roast venison
1 medium onion
100g/¹/₄lb diced cooked ham
150ml/¹/₄ pint rich game stock
450g/1lb cooked mashed potato
pinch of dried thyme

Pre-heat oven to 200°C/400°F/Gas Mark 6

1 Mince the venison and onion together and combine with the diced ham.

2 Put in a shallow ovenproof dish. Season well and add the pinch of thyme.

3 Heat the game stock to boiling and pour over the meat mixture.

4 Cover with the mashed potato and cook in a hot oven for about 20 minutes.

Venison Mireton

Serves 4

This classic leftovers dish is usually made with beef but venison is equally, if not more, tasty.

450g/1lb thinly sliced cold roast
*   venison*
2 large onions, finely chopped
1 clove crushed garlic
25g/1oz butter
25g/1oz flour
1 desert spoon wine vinegar
275ml/½ pint stock
1 tablespoon French whole grain
*   mustard*
1 tablespoon tomato purée

Pre-heat oven to 200°C/400°F/Gas mark 6.

---

1 Melt the butter and cook the onions and garlic until transparent, add the flour, stirring occasionally, then blend in the stock and vinegar until the sauce is thick and smooth.

---

2 Mix in the mustard and tomato purée and simmer gently for a further 10 minutes.

---

3 Put the thinly sliced venison into a shallow ovenproof dish and pour the sauce over. Cook for about 20 minutes in a hot oven.

---

4 This is good served with rice or creamed potatoes.

Venison Patties

Serves 4

450g/1lb cold roast venison
1 medium onion
1 beaten egg
pinch dried mixed herbs
1 teaspoon curry powder

1 Mince the meat and onion together, add the herbs and curry powder and mix well. Stir in the beaten egg.

2 Form the mixture into small patties and fry in a little heated cooking oil.

3 These can be served as 'burgers' for the children with mashed potato, a green vegetable and a home-made tomato sauce.

Italian Meat and Herb Sauce for Pasta

Serves 4–6

This rich, garlicky sauce can be made the night before – it makes a little meat go a long way and you can use it over noodles, tagliatelli or spaghetti.

225g/1/2lb cold cooked venison,
  minced
1 large onion, minced
2 cloves garlic, chopped
150g/6oz mushrooms, sliced
1 stick celery, chopped
4 ripe tomatoes, sliced
1 tablespoon tomato purée
2 tablespoons olive oil
150ml/1/4 pint rich meat stock
1 pinch oregano, sage and thyme

1 Heat the olive oil in a heavy-based pan. Add the onion, garlic and celery and cook until golden brown.

2 Now add the meat, mushrooms and tomatoes, tomato purée and herbs. Cook for 5 minutes, stirring well, then add the stock and simmer for about 20 minutes, seasoning to taste.

3 Serve over the selected pasta with grated cheese served separately.

Stuffed Pepper Islands

Serves 4

This is such an unusual and visually beautiful recipe that you might even be tempted to buy some venison instead of using the leftovers.

4 green peppers
225g/½lb cold, cooked venison,
*   minced or finely chopped*
100g/4oz cooked brown rice
100g/¼lb mushrooms, coarsely
*   chopped*
275ml/½ pint milk
2 eggs
50g/2oz grated cheese

Pre-heat oven to 180°C/350°F/Gas mark 4

1　Slice the stalk end from the peppers and clean thoroughly, removing all the seeds. Reserve top slices for later. Cut a small piece from the bottom of each pepper so that they will stand upright. This is quite important – peppers copying the leaning tower of Pisa will tip over during cooking and eject the filling.

2　Combine the venison, rice and mushrooms and season well. Use this mixture to stuff the cavity of each pepper.

3　Beat the eggs into the milk and pour into a shallow ovenproof dish. Arrange the peppers in this and put on the reserved top slices of the peppers to form a cap.

4　Sprinkle the grated cheese over – use a hard cheddar – and bake in a moderate oven for about 30–40 minutes until the cheese custard is golden.

5　Serve with grilled tomatoes and baked potatoes.

Stuffed Vegetable Medley

Serves 4

Even with a small amount of leftover venison you can stretch it to a substantial meal by making the following savoury or oriental stuffings to fill any vegetables you have available. You can use peppers, aubergines, courgettes or even potatoes, although with these you will need to bake them for an hour first.

Savoury Stuffing

325g/12oz cooked venison, minced
100g/4oz cooked brown rice
1 small onion, chopped finely
1 clove garlic, chopped finely
50g/2oz mushrooms, chopped
  coarsely
50g/2oz grated cheese
2 tomatoes, skinned and chopped
1 tablespoon chopped raisins
  (optional)
1 tablespoon chopped nuts (optional)
dash of olive oil
pinch dried oregano

1 Heat the olive oil in a large pan. Add the venison, rice, onion, garlic, mushrooms, tomatoes, nuts and raisins (if used) and oregano.

2 Stir gently for about 10 minutes to combine the flavours. Add the grated cheese and remove from the heat.

3 Prepare the chosen vegetables to provide a suitable cavity to put the stuffing in and fill them, pressing the stuffing down firmly.

4 Place in a shallow dish or roasting tin and surround with about ½in/1cm of hot water. Bake in a moderate oven for about ½ hour.

5 These are good served with a tomato sauce.

Oriental Stuffing

325g/12oz cooked venison, minced
225g/8oz cooked brown rice
2 eating apples, finely chopped
2 tablepoons mango chutney
2 teaspoons curry powder
1 teaspoon chopped cucumber
dash of olive oil

1 Combine all the ingredients in a bowl and prepare the chosen vegetables.

2 Pack the stuffing firmly into the cavities and cook as in the previous recipe.

3 This stuffing is especially good in aubergines, hollowed out lengthways.

Venison Hash

Serves 4–6

This is a slightly less calorific version of Mrs Beeton's famous hash recipe. She advocates using dripping for frying, but if you have none at hand or cannot bear the thought of so much instant cholesterol, then olive oil is a good substitute.

450g/1lb cooked venison, minced
1 medium onion, chopped
2 sticks celery, chopped
2 cloves garlic (not mentioned by Mrs
  Beeton)
1 tin of anchovies, chopped
1 medium tin tomatoes
4 medium potatoes, thinly sliced
1 tablespoon dripping, or
1 dessert spoon olive oil

Pre-heat oven to 200°C/400°F/Gas Mark 6

1 Heat the dripping or oil, onion, garlic and celery and cook for about 5 minutes.

2 Add the venison, tomatoes and anchovies and stir-fry for a further 5 minutes.

3 Transfer the mixture to a shallow ovenproof dish, cover with the sliced potatoes and drizzle the remaining anchovy oil over the top.

4 Bake in a hot oven for about 45 minutes until the potatoes are soft and golden brown.

CHAPTER 13
BARBECUES

Many venison cuts are excellent for barbecues with a difference, and relieve the boredom of yet another plate of burgers or chicken legs. Use the spicy marinade recommended in Chapter 2.

Foiled Rump Steaks

150g/6oz rump steak per person
spicy marinade
fresh thyme or rosemary (if available)

1 Marinade the steaks for a couple of hours and wrap each one in a loose foil
   parcel with a sprig of fresh herbs.

2 Lay on the hottest part of the barbecue and allow about 10 minutes cooking on
   each side.

Kebabs

Serves 4

700g/1½lb fillet or rump steak, cut
into cubes
100g/4oz mushrooms
1 green pepper, thickly sliced
1 large onion, thickly sliced
spicy marinade

1 Thread the meat onto skewers, alternating with the vegetables.

2 Brush with the marinade and lay on the cooler cooking end of the barbecue.

3 Turn frequently and with care and baste at intervals with more marinade.

Venison Sausages in Tomato Marinade

2 venison sausages per person

For the marinade:
150ml/¼ pint cooking oil
1 dessert spoon wine vinegar
1 clove crushed garlic
1 dessert spoon whole grain mustard
2 tablespoon tomato purée

1 Turn the sausages into the marinade and leave for at least 3 hours if possible before grilling.

2 Serve the sausages in a sesame seed bun or a hunk of French bread which can be spread with marinade.

Barbecued Kidneys

Allow 2 kidneys per person, preferably roe kidneys

1 Prepare the tomato marinade as in the previous recipe. Leave the kidney to marinade for 2–3 hours.

2 When ready to grill, wrap each kidney in a piece of streaky bacon – cook on the hottest part of the barbecue taking care not to overcook.

Barbecued Loin Chops

1 double chop per person, or
2 small chops per person

1 Marinade using the spicy marinade given in Chapter 2 for at least 2 hours.

2 Drain and place on a barbecue, turning frequently and basting from time to time with a litle oil on a pastry brush.

Note: If you have some fresh thyme or rosemary, then crumble these over the chops – it will give a delicious aromatic flavour.

Whole Fillet with Mushrooms and Honey

Serves 4

1 whole roe fillet, or
450g/1lb fallow fillet
spicy marinade
100g/¼lb whole button mushrooms
1 tablespoon honey

1 Marinade the fillet overnight or for a few hours for more impromptu feasts.

2 Lay on to a square of oiled foil. Spread with the honey and scatter over the mushrooms.

3 Put on the barbecue and cook on the hottest part for about 10 minutes only on each side.

Whole Spit Roast

Sometimes we are asked to give advice on cooking a whole venison carcass for a large barbecue. It provides a delicious and unusual centrepiece. Use a roe carcass if possible to ensure thorough cooking or a small, young fallow deer.

Make sure you have a barbecue fire which is long enough for the length of the meat! You do not want to finish up with cindered shoulders and raw haunches, so rig up some sort of spit to turn the meat frequently. Arm yourself with a large clean paintbrush and some cooking oil for frequent basting and away you go. Allow at least 8 hours for cooking.

CHAPTER 14

SMOKED VENISON

This is the most delicious and aromatic of all the smoked meats. If you are lucky enough to live near a source of local smoked foods, then ask for a thinly sliced, fresh cut smoked venison. If not, then you will have to rough it on packets of pre-sliced meat from a delicatessen.

Hors d'Oeuvres with Orange and Watercress

Serves 4

16 thin slices smoked venison
2 medium oranges, peeled and
  segmented with skin removed
1 bunch watercress to garnish

1 Alternate the slices of venison with the orange segments on individual plates.

2 Garnish each portion with a sprig of watercress – simple, but it looks quite stunning.

Smoked Venison with Cream Cheese and Green Pepper

Serves 4

8 large slices smoked venison
150g/6oz cream or curd cheese
1 green pepper, finely chopped
salt and pepper
lettuce leaves and redcurrant jelly to
garnish

1 Stir the green pepper and seasonings into the cream cheese. Place a little of this mixture on to the centre of each slice of venison and roll up into a cone.

2 Serve on a lettuce leaf with a small garnish of redcurrant jelly.

Smoked Venison with Rice Salad

Serves 4–6

This makes a wonderful, visual centrepiece for a cold, summer buffet.

12–18 slices smoked venison
450g/1lb cooked, cold brown rice
3 tablespoons olive oil
2 tablespoons red wine vinegar
1 dessert spoon fresh chopped parsley
1 dessert spoon fresh chopped lemon
   balm
1 dessert spoon finely chopped onion

**Plus choose any combination of
   the following:**
cooked green beans
artichoke hearts or peas
raw thin sliced carrot rounds
sliced radishes
diced celery
broccoli sprigs
cucumber strips
olives
tomato wedges and lemon segments
   to garnish

1 Season the rice and stir in the oil, vinegar, onion and herbs. If possible let it stand overnight to develop the flavours.

2 When ready to serve, combine the rice mixture with any of the chosen vegetables. Arrange in a mound on a large serving dish and surround with overlapping slices of smoked venison.

3 Garnish with tomato wedges and lemon segments and serve with crusty bread.

Smoked Venison with Quail's Eggs and Mixed Peppers

Serves 4

This is my favourite way to serve smoked venison – it is quite wonderful.

8–12 slices smoked venison
1 dozen quail's eggs
1 each small red, green and yellow
*   peppers*
4 lettuce leaves
1 tablespoon mayonnaise
parsley to garnish, or, even better
nasturtium flowers

1 Cover the quail's eggs with cold water, bring to the boil and cook for 4 minutes. Drain and leave to cool then shell and set aside.

2 Remove the seeds from the peppers and slice finely. Combine the quail's eggs with the sliced peppers and mayonnaise and season well.

3 To serve, lay the slices of smoked venison on individual plates. Place a heaped spoonful of the egg and pepper mixture on each lettuce leaf and lay alongside the venison.

4 Garnish with a sprig of parsley or if you have some, rush out into the garden for 4 nasturtium flowers with a single leaf.

Various Hors d'Oeuvres

Smoked venison combines so well with many vegetables and salads. Try the following or compose your own:

Sliced smoked venison with avocado slices.
Sliced smoked venison with grapefruit segments.
Sliced smoked venison with black olives and sliced tomatoes.
Sliced smoked venison with cold ratatouille.

We have concentrated on recipe ideas for the presentation of cold smoked venison. This last recipe is for a joint of hot, smoked, roast venison. It is the sort of dish that you could prepare when your guest of honour is a cordon bleu cook, a Michelin starred French chef, minor royalty or even a Roux brother. Rest assured they will not have tasted it before. It is clearly impressive and immensely easy.

Hot Smoked Venison Roast with Fruit Compote

Serves 6–8

1 haunch smoked venison, or
boneless haunch, boned and rolled
1 tablespoon crushed juniper berries
1 teaspoon grated lemon rind
pinch grated nutmeg
dash of olive oil
ground black pepper

For the fruit compote:
2 eating apples, peeled and thickly sliced
8 pitted prunes, pre-soaked
8 dried apricots, pre-soaked
1 large pear, peeled and thickly sliced
1 dessert spoon wine vinegar
1 pinch cinnamon
25g/1oz brown sugar

Pre-heat oven to 190°C/375°F/Gas mark 5.

---

1   Prepare the fruit compote – this is best done the day before or even 2 days
    before. Combine all the ingredients and simmer over a low heat for about ½ an
    hour, stirring occasionally. Remove from the heat, take out the cloves and set
    aside to cool.

---

2   Prepare the roast venison. Place the joint of meat on a large square of tin foil.
    Sprinkle with the juniper berries, lemon rind and nutmeg. Season with black
    pepper only – no salt. Drizzle over the olive oil and wrap into a loose parcel.

---

3   Roast in a moderate oven for 1 – 1½ hours. The meat should be pink in the
    middle like roast beef, so take care not to overcook it.

---

4   When ready to serve, slice the venison thinly on to a very hot serving dish.
    Heat the fruit compote and pass around separately.

---

5   Serve the venison with roast potatoes, red cabbage and a selection of root
    vegetables.

INDEX